The PIRATES of PENZANCE

or
THE SLAVE OF DUTY

Book by
W.S. Gilbert

Music by
Arthur Sullivan

Authentic Version Edited by
Bryceson Treharne

This score includes all the dialogue.

Orchestral material is available
on rental from G. Schirmer, Inc.

P.O. Box 572
445 Bellvale Road
Chester, NY 10918
(845) 469-2271
(845) 469-7544 (fax)
www.schirmer.com

Ed. 1655

ISBN 978-0-7935-2586-7

G. SCHIRMER, Inc.

DISTRIBUTED BY

HAL•LEONARD®
CORPORATION
7777 W. BLUEMOUND RD. P.O. BOX 13819 MILWAUKEE, WI 53213

DRAMATIS PERSONAE

Major-General Stanley

The Pirate King

Samuel . . . .*His Lieutenant*

Frederic . . . .*The Pirate Apprentice*

Sergeant of Police

Mabel . . . .⎫

Edith. . . . .⎪

Kate . . . .⎬ . . . .*Major-General Stanley's Wards*

Isabel . . . .⎭

Ruth . . . .*Pirate Maid-of-all-work*

Chorus of Pirates, Police, and General Stanley's Wards

ACT I—A Rocky Seashore on the Coast of Cornwall

ACT II—A Ruined Chapel by Moonlight

MUSICAL NUMBERS

ARGUMENT

When Frederic was yet a little boy, his nurse (Ruth) was told to apprentice him to become a pilot. She heard the word incorrectly and apprenticed him to a band of *pirates*, remaining with them as a maid-of-all-work. Although Frederic loathed the trade to which he had thus been bound, he dutifully served. As the curtain rises, his indentures are almost up and he is preparing to leave the band and devote himself to the extermination of piracy.

He urges the pirates to join him in embracing a more lawful calling, but they refuse. Ruth, however, wishes to become Frederic's wife. Having seen but few women, he does not know whether she is really as pretty as she says she is, but he he finally consents to take her.

Just then a group of girls, all the wards of Major-General Stanley, happen upon the scene. Frederic sees their beauty—and Ruth's plainness—and renounces her. Of these girls, Mabel takes a particular interest in Frederic, and he in her. The other girls are seized by the pirates and threatened with immediate marriage. When the Major-General arrives, he can dissuade the pirates only by a ruse: he tells them that he is an orphan, and so works upon their sympathies that they let him and his wards go free.

During the ensuing days and nights, however, this lie troubles the Major-General's conscience; he sits brooding over it at night in a Gothic ruin. He is consoled by his wards' sympathy and Frederic's plan of immediately leading a band of police against the pirates.

Meanwhile, the Pirate King and Ruth appear at the window and beckon Frederic. They have discovered that his indentures were to run until his twenty-first birthday, and—as he was born on February 29—he has really had as yet only five birthdays. Obeying the dictates of his strong sense of duty, he immediately rejoins the pirates. He tells them of the deception that has been practiced upon them, and they seize and bind the Major-General.

But the police come to the rescue and charge the pirates to yield, "in Queen Victoria's name." This they do. Ruth explains, however, that these men who appear to be lawless pirates are really "noblemen who have gone wrong," and they are pardoned and permitted to marry the Major-General's wards.

GILBERT&SULLIVAN

W.S. Gilbert

Arthur Sullivan

THE GILBERT & SULLIVAN PARTNERSHIP
By Marie Eggold

In fourteen operettas over the course of twenty-five years, W.S. Gilbert and Arthur Sullivan etched their names in the history books forever. Their works not only created an English school of light opera, they whetted an appetite for musical theater in the United States and around the world. Their works have inspired a steady stream of recordings, revivals, books and articles over the past century, with films and web sites appearing more recently. Gilbert and Sullivan have remained at the heart of the operetta repertoire for more than 100 years. Yet for Gilbert, who aspired to write serious dramas, and Sullivan, who aspired to write serious music, writing entertainment for the Victorian middle class was not quite fulfilling.

Although one seldom hears the names Gilbert and Sullivan spoken separately, the two had careers independent of one another. They were also remarkably different men. Gilbert was well over six feet tall and fair complected, with a rather grim face. Sullivan on the other hand was quite short, dark haired and was known for an easy smile and twinkling eyes. As Gilbert aged, he retained a youthful vigor that allowed him to show off occasional dance steps in his later years, just to prove that he still could. Sullivan's health was poor. He was stricken with a painful kidney ailment and walked with a cane while still a young man. Gilbert was regarded as one of the most prominent dramatists of his day, while Sullivan was seen as someone with a tremendous gift that he failed to develop fully.

William Schwenck Gilbert

William Schwenck Gilbert was born on November 18, 1836, just a few months before the reign of Queen Victoria began. His father, Dr. William Gilbert, had served as a naval surgeon until an inheritance allowed him to retire to travel and write. In later years the younger Gilbert, called Schwenck by his family, would illustrate some of his father's publications. Schwenck studied law and practiced briefly, but soon turned his attention to writing. He was a frequent contributor to *Fun* magazine, publishing drawings, short stories, and dramatic criticism. Best remembered of his work from this time are the *Bab Ballads*, stories in verse that he signed with his childhood nickname. The name is short for "Babby," his family's twist on baby.

Topics and ideas from the *Bab Ballads* and other early works show up, fleshed out, in the operettas, as do several recurring themes. The Gilbert family often told the story of how Schwenck had been kidnapped while they were in Italy. He was only missing for a few hours, quickly returned for a small bit of money. But he claimed to have a memory of the event, likely just familiarity from hearing the tale repeated throughout his childhood. The idea of two children switched at birth, and the ensuing crisis of identity and social class, pops up again and again in his works, most notably in *The Pirates of Penzance*. Another theme was one of topsy-turvy worlds. Gilbert was fascinated by plots and scenarios based on things being just the opposite of what they should be. Virtue was evil, peace was war etc. He explored the idea in his one-act extravaganza, *Topsyturveydom*, which opened on March 21, 1874, returning to it throughout his career. By the mid-1870s, Gilbert was well-known as a playwright.

From the first "official" biography of Gilbert, which appeared in 1923, to the 1935 Hesketh Pearson book *Gilbert and Sullivan*, and his 1957 *Gilbert–His Life and Strife*, William Schwenck Gilbert was painted as a kindly, fairly typical British gentleman. In fact, Gilbert was a very difficult man. "I am an ill-tempered pig," he once wrote, "and I glory in it." In the book *Between Ourselves* (1930), Seymour Hicks wrote of Gilbert, "He always gave me the impression that he got up in the morning to see with whom he could have a quarrel." Indeed, Gilbert seemed to relish quarrels. He was an extremely litigious man. He saw personal slights at every turn and was not content until things were put right, in his favor of course. His stock line in such situations was, "I shall place the matter at once in the hands of my solicitor."

Arthur Sullivan

Arthur Sullivan, on the other hand, was a kind, likeable man with no great ego. He enjoyed having fun and was somewhat notorious for his various appetites, which included incessant travel, encounters with prostitutes, and constant indulging in fine foods and wines. He was born on May 13, 1842, to a bandmaster who filled his son's life with music and recognized the boy's talents early. By 1856, Arthur was a scholarship student at the Royal Academy of Music, studying at the Leipzig Conservatory from 1858 to 1861. His instructors there believed he had a greater musical gift than Brahms. Later it was said that he had greater ability than any English musician since Purcell. In the face of such lavish praise, his work in operettas, no matter how popular and successful they might be, was viewed by critics as a waste of a tremendous talent.

A conductor, educator, and organist, in addition to being a composer, Sullivan had written a good deal of "serious" music by the time he began his partnership with Gilbert. He always viewed his theater work as secondary to serious composition, which included choral works, a symphony, a ballet and numerous hymns, the most famous being "Onward Christian Soldiers." Yet an article that appeared in the *Pall Mall Gazette* at the time of the premiere of *The Gondoliers* declared Sullivan England's most popular composer—popularity won by operettas. The same biographers who overlooked Gilbert's irascible nature treated Sullivan's easy-going personality and voracious appetites harshly.

The recipient of several honorary doctorates, Sullivan was not an intellectual, nor was he a literary man. He was, however, remembered by colleagues as a remarkable wit. Perhaps his greatest musical gift was his uncanny ability to contrive music to fit any lyric, any scene, and any mood. His music became an integral part of the theatrical scene, not a separate element. He would tailor his melodies to Gilbert's pattering poetry, gild a tune to match the sets or dances of a particular scene, and orchestrate the entire thing with grace and good humor.

The Partnership

The Gilbert and Sullivan partnership was actually a trio. The third partner was Richard D'Oyly Carte, who served as the catalyst who made the creative pair household names. Carte was the son of Richard Carte, a flautist and partner in the musical instrument manufacturing firm of Rudall, Carte and Co. He started out in his father's business, wrote some operettas and conducted as well. But by the time he was twenty-five, he had set up his own theatrical and concert agency. Carte was not involved in Gilbert and Sullivan's first collaboration, *Thespis, or The Gods Grown Old*, which opened at the Gaiety Theatre on December 26, 1871. The libretto and score were never published and all but two numbers have been lost. Carte brought the writers together for *Trial By Jury*, which opened at the Royalty Theatre on March 25, 1875, performed with two other pieces. It outlived the productions with which it shared a bill and set Carte in motion. He interested several investing partners, leased the Opera Comique and announced the creation of the Comedy Opera Company. The company produced *The Sorcerer*, which opened on October 17, 1877, and *H.M.S. Pinafore*, which opened on May 25, 1878. Although *Pinafore* had opened to receptive audiences and positive reviews, an unusually hot summer kept people out of the theaters and began a rift between Carte and the investors that eventually led to their separation. This left Carte free to form a partnership with the librettist and composer. The company was first known as Mr. D'Oyly Carte's Company until the name was changed to The D'Oyly Carte Opera Company in 1889. With Carte at the helm, Gilbert and Sullivan created *The Pirates of Penzance*, which opened in England on December 30, 1879 and in New York a day later. *Patience* followed, opening in London on April 23, 1881.

Carte then built the Savoy Theatre in London, devoted to the production of the work of Gilbert and Sullivan. Erected on the site of the palace of Savoy that had been destroyed in the late 1300s, it was a strikingly modern theater. In fact, it was the world's first theater to be completely lit by electricity. With electricity came the ability to create lighting effects, which helped draw audiences to productions. A generator located in an empty lot beside the theater provided the power. A few years later Carte opened the Savoy Hotel on that lot, which was also a progressive building at the time. The Savoy Theatre hosted the premieres of *Iolanthe* in 1882, *Princess Ida* in 1884, *The Mikado* in 1885, *Ruddigore* in 1887, *The Yeoman of the Guard* in 1888, *The Gondoliers* in 1889, *Utopia Limited* in 1893, and *The Grand Duke* in 1896.

The Ocean Was Not Always Blue

Despite the levity of the operettas, the partnership was not bliss. Carte was building a new theater, the Royal English Opera House, in which he intended to premiere Sullivan's grand opera, *Ivanhoe*. Although the January 31, 1891 premiere was received with accolades, the public was not ready to embrace grand opera as it had embraced light opera. Carte eventually sold the theater. Meanwhile, as *Ruddigore* was running and Sullivan was preparing *Ivanhoe*, Gilbert took a close look at the accounts for the partnership. He found an expense of £140 to re-carpet the Savoy lobby and took offense. He felt that he and Sullivan should not be charged for such an extravagance. Sullivan sided with Carte. What ensued, remembered as the famous Carpet Quarrel, created a wound that would not heal. The partnership was dissolved. Eventually the trio put their differences aside and created *Utopia Limited* and *The Grand Duke*, but things were never the same. Even in the best of times, Gilbert and Sullivan referred to each other by their surnames. Gilbert was constantly at war with one or another cast member, making rehearsals awkward affairs by giving his undivided attention to everyone but the party at whom he was angry. When the offending actor did a scene, Gilbert would pointedly ignore the goings-on, turning his back to the stage and making a great show of talking to someone until the scene was over.

Following *The Gondoliers*, the Savoy was largely devoted to revivals of Gilbert and Sullivan's operettas, or to pieces written by Sullivan with another librettist. But the partnership Gilbert/Sullivan/D'Oyly Carte would not have survived the 1890s regardless of the Carpet Quarrel. Both Sullivan and Carte were in failing health. Sullivan's health had been in a long decline, his kidney disease causing him horrendous pain. He died on November 22, 1900. Carte survived him by just six months. Gilbert however, maintained a vigorous lifestyle to the end. On May 29, 1911 the seventy-four-year-old Gilbert endeavored to teach two women to swim in the lake he had created at his home. When one of the women floundered, Gilbert dove in to save her, suffering a fatal heart attack in the water.

The Legacy

The magic of the Gilbert and Sullivan partnership lay in the cutting wit and perfectionism of Gilbert, who micro-managed details of rehearsals, and his ability to craft a plot of many convoluted layers, only to have it all sort out neatly in the end. Along the way he would poke fun at social conventions, the law, and romance. Sullivan was the one who made froth of this wit. He could craft melodies that instantly projected the dramatic intent of Gilbert's lines. He was fearless in his treatment of rhythms. He rose to such challenges as setting the mouthfuls of lyrics presented by "I am the Very Model of a Modern Major General," creating an operetta classic. Their contributions did not go unrecognized. Sullivan was knighted in 1883. Gilbert was knighted in 1907.

The D'Oyly Carte Opera Company continued presenting and touring the works of Gilbert and Sullivan until financial difficulties forced it to close in 1982. The D'Oyly Carte Opera Trust had been formed in 1961, when the copyrights ran out on the operettas. In her will, Dame Bridget Carte left £1 million to the trust, earmarking it to reform the company. The company reappeared in 1988, returning to the Savoy Theatre in 2000.

THE PIRATES OF PENZANCE
By Marie Eggold

The story of the creation and premiere of W.S. Gilbert and Arthur Sullivan's *The Pirates of Penzance, or The Slave of Duty*, reads a bit like one of Gilbert's comically convoluted plots. The premiere, or more accurately premieres, of the operetta took place on opposite sides of the Atlantic, on December 30 and 31, 1879. But the story begins much earlier.

Due to the lack of international copyright laws in the late 1800s, the work of composers and authors was routinely pirated, or presented in productions or reprints without the creator's consent. This of course meant that authors or composers received no royalties for these pirated productions or copies. Gilbert and Sullivan were hit particularly hard by this problem. *H.M.S. Pinafore* was such a success in England that numerous companies in America presented productions that were not only unauthorized, but often quite unlike the original because they were based on inaccurate, pirated librettos and scores. This was especially galling for Gilbert, who insisted on having tight control over the D'Oyly Carte productions of his works. He went so far as to seek out untrained actors for his productions, preferring to teach them their craft as rehearsals progressed, thereby insuring his control.

By mid-1879, as Carte, Gilbert and Sullivan progressed with the creation of a new operetta, the flood of pirated American productions of *H.M.S. Pinafore* became a critical issue. The only way to control the copyright of a new show in America was to give the show's official premiere in that country, keeping the libretto and music tightly under wraps until opening night. It was decided that Gilbert, Sullivan and Carte would set up shop in New York for a few months to present an authorized version of *H.M.S. Pinafore*, and to open what would become *The Pirates of Penzance* shortly thereafter.

Gilbert and Sullivan sailed for New York, arriving on November 5, 1879, with Carte and several actors arriving on November 11. Once in the U.S., the partners hit the ground running. The first order of business was to set up the *Pinafore* production. The production opened at the Fifth Avenue Theatre on December 1. But American audiences had seen enough of *Pinafore*, thanks to the abundance of unauthorized productions, and revenues from the New York *Pinafore* were not what Carte had predicted. About a week after the opening, the decision was made to move up the premiere of the new show, which would also play the Fifth Avenue Theatre. As late as August of that year, the working title was *The Robbers*. It is not clear just when Gilbert made the switch to a piracy theme, but there is some speculation that it was a tongue-in-cheek comment on the various pirated productions of *Pinafore*.

Gilbert, having brought actors from England to play leading roles in *Pirates*, had to hire an American chorus. As always, he was seeking actors he could train and control. To that end he posted an advertisement saying, "amateurs, desirous of adopting the lyric stage, should report to Steinway Hall and ask for Mr. R. D'Oyly Carte." He added that they must have good voices and a knowledge of music, and must be young and attractive. Several hundred hopefuls showed up for the audition.

Gilbert was hiring, and eventually rehearsing, actors for a show that was not yet complete. Sullivan, whose penchant for procrastination was legendary, was working nights, often all through the night, to get *Pirates* completed, while rehearsing the existing music during the day. All the while he was suffering from an attack of the painful kidney disease that plagued him. To complicate matters, he realized that he had left his Act I sketches in England. There was no longer time to cable home and have them sent, so he began rewriting the first act from memory. This may be why he borrowed "Climbing over rocky mountain" from his first collaboration with Gilbert, *Thespis*. The piece exists in his *Pirates* autograph score, housed at the Pierpont Morgan Library, with the *Thespis* lyrics crossed out and *Pirates* lyrics written in. He also changed the vocal parts from a standard four-part arrangement to parts for women only. Thanks to this borrowing, it is one of only two musical selections from *Thespis* that have survived. The debate still rages among scholars as to whether Sullivan intended from the outset to include "Climbing over rocky mountain" in *Pirates* or if he happened to have the music with him and simply slipped it in to save some time. Whatever the case, the score was finished, although minus the overture, at 7 A.M., December 28, and was taken straight to a rehearsal.

Gilbert was also borrowing from his earlier work to create *Pirates*. Although some critics complained that *Pirates* was just "*H.M.S. Pinafore* on dry land," or "the third act of *H.M.S. Pinafore*," it actually was a unique show with roots that had nothing to do with the pair's previous production. The libretto is very closely related to Gilbert's 1870 play, *Our Island Home*. That show also featured a pirate King, whom Gilbert named Captain Bang, and the plot device of someone being sent off on an apprenticeship as a pirate rather than as a pilot. It was not, however, set in Penzance, an actual Cornish seaside resort town that really was plagued by attacking Mediterranean pirates until about 1800. Another reason for a second operetta based on swashbuckling themes was the general popularity of pirates and sea adventures in Victorian England. Robert Louis Stevenson's *Treasure Island* was published in 1883. Gilbert himself had translated Offenbach's *Les Brigands*, a three-act operetta with a similar theme, in 1871. In addition, the plot elements common to *Pinafore* and *Pirates*—a pair of young lovers, a villain and a comedic character of some sort—were part of a theatrical tradition that had its roots in pantomime. They were elements that Victorian audiences had come to expect in comedies.

Meanwhile, the press was literally listening at the doors of the theater, desperate for any news or hints about the new show, as were those hoping to steal it. Carte, Gilbert and Sullivan worked in constant fear of the score being pirated before opening night. By American law, once a show appeared in print it became public domain. To protect the work, Carte had guards posted at the theater entrances, allowing only people directly involved in the production into the building. No librettos or orchestral parts were allowed out of the theater. In fact, they were kept under lock and key when not in the hands of actors and musicians. Gilbert broke with the tradition of handing out librettos, fearing they would fall into the wrong hands either before or after the opening. Bribes were offered to performers to get copies of the libretto or music, but no one sold out. In order to keep producers in outlying areas from being tempted to present unauthorized productions of *Pirates*, Carte, Gilbert and Sullivan quickly arranged for several touring companies to take the show to the hinterlands. But even with these extraordinary precautions and efforts, *Pirates* was pirated. Copyists were in the audience on opening night, and many nights thereafter. After each hearing they would write out as much as they could remember, until they had a reasonably complete, if not correct, version of the show in hand. It was published in America under the title, *Recollections of the Pirates of Penzance*, long before the official printed version was available.

Although the musicians of the *Pirates* orchestra were loyal in refusing bribes, they were not so loyal as concerned their own pay scale. A few days before the New York premiere of *Pirates*, the orchestra declared that the score was not so much a light opera as a grand opera. Since the pay for grand opera was higher than for operetta, they thought it only fair that they be paid the higher wage. They informed Sullivan that they would strike rather than accept the lower operetta pay. What they didn't bargain for was Sullivan's gambling nature. He took their comments in stride, thanking them for thinking so highly of his score. He then bluffed, announcing that he had just finished conducting an engagement with the Covent Garden orchestra and could cable them to sail for America immediately. In the interim he and conductor Alfred Cellier would be more than happy to accompany the performances on piano and harmonium. He then requested an interview with one of the New York newspapers and told the story to the press. The musicians, who didn't fare well in the newspaper account, took him at his word and backed down. In the midst of this mayhem, actress Helen Everard, playing the part of Ruth, was injured in one of the final rehearsals when a piece of scenery fell on her. She suffered a fractured skull and eventually died of the injury. Actress Emily Cross stepped in on twenty-four hours notice.

The haste and flurry of activity surrounding the American premiere of *Pirates* paled significantly in comparison to the British premiere, hastily given to establish copyright in England. The town of Paignton, in Devon, was chosen for the premiere, partly because the town was home to the Royal Bijou Theatre, and partly because there was a touring company of *Pinafore* in the area that could be pressed into service to give a single performance of the new work. But *Pirates* was not done, and furthermore, was across the Atlantic and not available for rehearsal. The performance was originally scheduled for December 29, but had to be postponed by a day because the music had not arrived from New York. In the end, the *Pinafore* company presented an incomplete, sketchy version of *Pirates*, accompanied by piano, at 2 P.M. on December 30. It played to an audience of fifty. The production was supervised by Helen Lenoir, Carte's right-hand person who later became his wife. Cast members had one rehearsal under their belts, and had to wear their *Pinafore* costumes, which meant that the policemen were dressed as soldiers and the pirates as navy men. They carried their parts on stage, reading lines and music throughout the performance. The piano accompaniment was incomplete, the most notable omission being the overture, which Sullivan did not begin until 16 hours before the curtain was to rise on the New York premiere. Both "Poor Wand'ring One" and "Come Lads Who Plough the Sea" were missing from the Paignton performance because they too were not completed in time to send across the Atlantic.

Gilbert, Sullivan and Carte stayed in the United States long enough to set up three touring companies of *Pirates*. Gilbert rehearsed the actors and Sullivan conducted openings on February 9 in Philadelphia, on February 16 in Newark, and on February 21 in Buffalo. In the weeks that followed he presented some of his music in concert and traveled to Canada, where he was the guest of Queen Victoria's daughter, Princess Louise. Carte, Gilbert and Sullivan sailed for London on March 3, 1880, to prepare for the London premiere of *Pirates*. Their American visit had been a huge success. "Come Lads who plough the sea" was quickly appropriated by Americans with the lyrics "Hail, hail the gang's all here." A plaque was mounted at 45 East 20th Street in New York, at the hotel where Gilbert and Sullivan had stayed while working on *Pirates*, announcing, "On this site Sir Arthur Sullivan composed 'The Pirates of Penzance' in 1879."

Pirates opened at the Opera Comique in London on April 3, 1880, where it ran for over 400 performances, an enormous success in those days. While the humor of the plot and the topsy-turviness of sherry-sipping pirates and policemen who loathe confrontation were apparent to American audiences, the British most appreciated the temperament of the show's humor. The character of the Major-General is thought to have been a spoof of Sir Garnet Wolseley, a prominent British military hero of the African campaigns. The actor playing the role was given a mustache similar to Wolseley's and was told to imitate him. The additional satires of the police and unquestioning loyalty to the Queen, or to a painting of her, also tickled the British. Gilbert demanded that the roles be played straight, as though the performers were unaware of the ridiculous nature of the goings on. Never one to miss a marketing opportunity, Carte organized a children's production of *Pirates* in 1884; the performers ranged in age from ten to thirteen. *Pirates* was revived at the Savoy Theatre in the 1900-1901 season and again in the 1908-1909 season. A new production of *Pirates* opened the newly refurbished Savoy Theatre in 1929.

In the United States, lines from *Pirates* found their way into everyday speech, much the way lines from popular television shows and films do today. Police were frequently greeted with a jovial "A policeman's lot is not a happy one." "Come lads who plough the sea" was appropriated by prohibitionists, fitted with lyrics to support their cause. On June 20, 1939, *Pirates* appeared on one of the first experimental broadcasts of the new medium of television. It remains one of the most popular, if not the most popular, of the Gilbert and Sullivan operettas.

THE PIRATES OF PENZANCE
Selected Discography

Recommended recordings:

1. The 1929 D'Oyly Carte recording conducted by Sir Malcolm Sargent, first issued as 78 RPM recording by HMV, followed by RCA Victor in 1930, reissued on LP by Pearl in 1979, Arabesque in 1981; reissued on CD by EMI in 1982, by Arabesque in 1986, by Pro Arte in 1992, by Happy Days in 1995, by Romophone in 1996, and by J. C. Lockwood 78s to CD in 2000. Major-General Stanley: George Baker; Pirate King: Peter Dawson; Samuel: Stuart Robertson; Frederic: Derek Oldham; Sergeant of Police: Leo Sheffield; Mabel: Elsie Griffin; Edith: Nellie Briercliffe; Kate: Nellie Walker; Ruth: Dorothy Gill

2. The 1957 D'Oyly Carte recording conducted by Isidore Godfrey, issued on LP in 1958 by Decca and London, with excerpted highlights released in a few months later. Major-General Stanley: Peter Pratt; Pirate King: Donald Adams; Samuel: Howard Short; Frederic: Thomas Round; Sergeant of Police: Kenneth Sandford; Mabel: Jean Hindmarsh; Edith: Beryl Dixon; Kate: Marian Martin; Ruth: Ann Drummond-Grant

3. The 1961 Glyndebourne recording conducted by Sir Malcolm Sargent, issued on LP by EMI in 1961 and again in 1969; also released on LP on the Angel label in the 1960s and 1970s; a digitally re-mastered LP was released by EMI/Angel in 1985; an EMI CD with other G&S overtures released in 1989 and again in 1992; an HMV CD released in 1998, part of a 16-disc set containing all nine of the Sargent/Glyndebourne G&S recordings with various Sullivan orchestral pieces in 2001. Major-General Stanley: George Baker; Pirate King: James Milligan; Samuel: John Cameron; Frederic: Richard Lewis; Sergeant of Police: Owen Brannigan; Mabel: Elsie Morison; Edith: Heather Harper; Kate: Marjorie Thomas; Ruth: Monica Sinclair

4. The 1962 highlights recording conducted by Alex Faris, issued on LP by World Record Club Limited; released subsequently on various other labels. Major-General Stanley: Patrick Halstead; Pirate King: William Dickie; Samuel: Christopher Keyte; Frederic: Edward Darling; Sergeant of Police: John Gower; Mabel: Elizabeth Harwood; Edith: Barbara Elsy; Kate: Patricia Beech; Ruth: Noreen Willett

5. The 1968 D'Oyly Carte recording, conducted by Isidore Godfrey, issued on LP by Decca and London in 1968; a digitally re-mastered LP released by Decca in 1984; a London CD released in 1990; highlights on London and Decca released in 1993. Major-General Stanley: John Reed; Pirate King: Donald Adams; Samuel: George Cook; Frederic: Philip Potter; Sergeant of Police: Owen Brannigan; Mabel: Valerie Masterson; Edith: Jean Allister; Kate: Pauline Wales; Isabel: Susan Maisey; Ruth: Christene Palmer

6. The 1981 Joseph Papp Broadway production, issued on LP by Electra; released on CD in 1998. Major-General Stanley: George Rose; Pirate King: Kevin Kline; Samuel: Stephan Hanan; Frederic: Rex Smith; Sergeant of Police: Tony Azito; Mabel: Linda Ronstadt; Edith: Alexandra Korey; Kate: Marcie Shaw; Isabel: Wendy Wolfe; Ruth: Estelle Parsons

7. The 1990 New D'Oyly Carte recording, conducted by John Pryce-Jones, features the reorganized D'Oyly Carte Company, issued on CD in 1990 by Sony and TER; released by Showtime in 1994; highlights versions were issued by Boots and Showtime in 1992 and by Koch in 1994. Major-General Stanley: Eric Roberts; Pirate King: Malcolm Rivers; Samuel: Gareth Jones; Frederic: Philip Creasy; Sergeant of Police: Simon Masterton Smith; Mabel: Marilyn Hill Smith; Edith: Patricia Cameron; Kate: Pauline Birchall; Isabel: Juliet Arthur; Ruth: Susan Gorton

8. The 1993 Welsh National Opera and Chorus recording, conducted by Sir Charles Mackerras, released on CD by Telarc in 1993; released by Telarc in 1999 as a set with the other four Mackerras G&S recordings, performed without overtures. Major-General Stanley: Richard Suart; Pirate King: Donald Adams; Samuel: Nicholas Folwell; Frederic: John Mark Ainsley; Sergeant of Police: Richard Van Allan; Mabel: Rebecca Evans; Edith: Julie Gossage; Kate: Jenevora Williams; Ruth: Gillian Knight

THE PIRATES OF PENZANCE
Filmography and Videography

1972, *The Pirates of Penzance*, film and companion recording by the Gilbert and Sullivan For All touring company, conducted by Peter Murray; Major-General Stanley: John Cartier; Pirate King: Donald Adams; Samuel: Michael Wakeham; Frederic: Thomas Round; Sergeant of Police: Lawrence Richard; Mabel: Valerie Masterson; Edith: Anna Cooper; Kate: Vera Ryan; Isabel: Elizabeth Lowry; Ruth: Helen Landis

1980, *The Pirates of Penzance* Joseph Papp production, video of the original Central Park run before moving to Broadway, directed by Wilford Leach, William Elliott, musical director. Major-General Stanley: George Rose; Pirate King: Kevin Kline; Samuel: G. Eugene Moose; Frederic: Rex Smith; Sergeant of Police: Tony Azito; Mabel: Linda Ronstadt; Edith: Alice Playten; Kate: Marcie Shaw; Isabel: Wendy Wolfe; Ruth: Patricia Routledge

1982, *The Pirate Movie*, a send-up of the operetta intended for a teen audience, directed by Ken Annakin. Major-General Stanley: Bill Kerr; Pirate King: Ted Hamilton; Samuel: Chuck McKinney; Frederic: Christopher Atkins; Sergeant/Inspector: Garry McDonald; Mabel: Kristy McNichol; Edith: Kate Ferguson; Kate: Rhonda Burchmore; Isabel: Cathrine Lynch; Ruth: Maggie Kirkpatrick

1982, Brent Walker Productions video of *Pirates*, featuring the Ambrosian Opera Chorus, the London Symphony Orchestra and Alexander Faris conducting, directed by Michael Geliot, issued by Brent Walker in 1982, Pioneer Artists in 1983, Woolworth in 1986, BraveWorld Video in 1991, Polygram Video in 1994, Opera World in 1996 and Roadshow in 1999. Major-General Stanley: Keith Michell; Pirate King: Peter Allen; Samuel: Brian Donlan; Frederic: Alexander Oliver; Sergeant of Police: Paul Hudson; Mabel: Janis Kelly; Edith: Kate Flowers; Kate: Jenny Wren; Ruth: Gillian Knight

1983, *The Pirates of Penzance*, film based on Joseph Papp's Broadway adaptation of the opera, directed by Wilford Leach, *musical director* William Elliott; Major-General Stanley: George Rose; Pirate King: Kevin Kline; Samuel: David Hatton; Frederic: Rex Smith; Sergeant of Police: Tony Azito; Mabel: Linda Ronstadt; Edith: Louise Gold (voice of Alexandra Korey); Kate: Teresa Codling (voice of Marcie Shaw); Isabel: Wendy Wolfe; Ruth: Angela Lansbury

1994, *The Pirates of Penzance*, Essgee Entertainment, video of the hit production of Australia and New Zealand, directed by Craig Schaefer. Major-General Stanley: Derek Metzger; Pirate King: Jon English; Samuel: Marc James; Frederic: Simon Gallagher; Sergeant of Police: Tim Tyler (Australia), David Gould (New Zealand); Mabel: Helen Donaldson; Major-General's Daughters (The Fabulous Singlettes): Anna Butera, Susie French, Melissa Langton, Ruth Toni Lamond (Australia), Bev Shean (New Zealand)

GILBERT'S "BAB" ILLUSTRATIONS

W. S. Gilbert's nickname as a child was "Bab," the family's shortened form for baby.
He illustrated each of his librettos with drawings, signed with "Bab." These are some
of his illustrations for *The Pirates of Penzance*.

Pirate with blunderboss.

Frederick, in the line,
"Pour, oh, pour the pirate sherry;
Fill, oh, fill the pirate glass."

Mabel, singing
"Poor wandering one."

Samuel sings, "For death prepare, unhappy General Stanley."

"Sad the lot of poplar trees, courted by a fickle breeze!"

Ruth sings, "I was a stupid nurserymaid, on breakers always steering."

"A policeman's lot is not a happy one."

"I am the very model of a
modern Major-General."

The Pirates of Penzance

or
The Slave of Duty

W. S. Gilbert

Arthur Sullivan

Overture

88710 r

Allegro vivace

Act I

Scene: *A rocky seashore on the coast of Cornwall. In the distance is a calm sea, on which a schooner is lying at anchor. Rocks L. sloping down to L.C. of stage. Under these rocks is a cavern, the entrance to which is seen at first entrance L. A natural arch of rock occupies the R.C. of the stage. As the curtain rises, groups of pirates are discovered— some drinking, some playing cards. Samuel, the pirate lieutenant, is going from one group to another, filling the cups from a flask. Frederic is seated in a despondent attitude at the back of the scene, C. Ruth kneels at his feet.*

No. 1. "Pour, O pour the pirate sherry"
Opening Chorus and Solo
Pirates and Samuel

Chorus
TENORS

Pour, O pour the pi - rate sher- ry; Fill, O fill the pi - rate glass;

BASSES

Pour, O pour the pi - rate sher-ry; Fill, O fill the pi - rate glass;

And, to make us more than

And, to make us more than

mer- ry, Let the pi - rate bum-per pass.

mer- ry, Let the pi - rate bum-per pass.

Sam.

Two - and - twen - ty, now he's ris - ing,

And a - lone he's fit to fly, Which we're bent on

sig - nal - iz - ing With un - u - sual rev - el - ry.

Chorus

Here's good luck_ to Fred-'ric's ven - tures! Fred-'ric's out of his in-den-tures.

Here's good luck_ to Fred-'ric's ven - tures! Fred-'ric's out of his in-den-tures.

(Frederic rises and comes forward with Pirate King, who enters from R.U.E.)

King: Yes, Frederic, from to-day you rank as a full-blown member of our band.

All: Hurrah!

Fred.: My friends, I thank you all, from my heart, for your kindly wishes. Would that I could repay them as they deserve!

King: What do you mean?

Fred.: To-day I am out of my indentures, and to-day I leave you forever.

King: But this is quite unaccountable; a keener hand at scuttling a Cunarder or cutting out a White Star never shipped a handspike.

Fred.: Yes, I have done my best for you. And why? It was my duty under my indentures, and I am the slave of duty. As a child I was regularly apprenticed to your band. It was through an error— no matter, the mistake was ours, not yours, and I was in honour bound by it.

Sam.: An error? What error? *(Ruth rises and comes forward.)*

Fred.: I may not tell you; it would reflect upon my well-loved Ruth.

Ruth: Nay, dear master, my mind has long been gnawed by the cankering tooth of mystery. Better have it out at once.

No. 2. "When Frederic was a little lad"
Solo
Ruth

Fred - 'ric was a __ lit - tle lad he __ proved so brave and
was a stu - pid __ nurs - 'ry - maid, on __ break - ers al - ways
soon found out, be - yond all doubt, the __ scope of this dis -

life not bad for a har-dy lad, though sure-ly not a high lot, Though
sad mis-take it__ was to make, and doom him to a vile lot, I
that is how you find me now, a__ mem-ber of your shy lot, Which you

I'm a nurse, you might do worse than make your boy a pi-lot!
bound him to a pi-rate—you!— in-stead of to a pi-lot!
would-n't have found, had he been bound ap-pren-tice to a pi-lot!

After 3rd verse

Ruth: Oh, pardon! Frederic, pardon! *(Kneels.)*

Fred.: Rise, sweet one; I have long pardoned you. *(Ruth rises.)*

Ruth: The two words were so much alike!

Fred.: They were. They still are, though years have rolled over their heads. *(Ruth goes up with Samuel.)* But this afternoon my obligation ceases. Individually, I love you all with affection unspeakable; but, collectively, I look upon you with a disgust that amounts to absolute detestation. Oh! pity me, my beloved friends, for such is my sense of duty that, once out of my indentures, I shall feel myself bound to devote myself heart and soul to your extermination!

All: Poor lad! poor lad! *(All weep.)*

King: Well, Frederic, if you conscientiously feel that it is your duty to destroy us, we cannot blame you for acting on that conviction. Always act in accordance with the dictates of your conscience, my boy, and chance the consequences.

Sam.: Besides, we can offer you but little temptation to remain with us. We don't seem to make piracy pay. I'm sure I don't know why, but we don't.

Fred.: *I* know why, but, alas! I mustn't tell you: it wouldn't be right.

King: Why not, my boy? It's only half-past eleven, and you are one of us until the clock strikes twelve.

Sam.: True, and until then you are bound to protect our interests.

All: Hear, hear!

Fred.: Well, then, it is my duty, as a pirate, to tell you that you are too tender-hearted. For instance, you make a point of never attacking a weaker party than yourselves, and when you attack a stronger party you invariably get thrashed.

King: There is some truth in that.

Fred.: Then, again, you make a point of never molesting an orphan.

Sam.: Of course: we are orphans ourselves, and know what it is.

Fred.: Yes, but it has got about, and what is the consequence? Every one we capture says he's an orphan. The last three ships we took proved to be manned entirely by orphans, and so we had to let them go. One would think that Great Britain's mercantile navy was recruited solely from her orphan asylums— which we know is not the case. (*Crosses R.*)

Sam.: But, hang it all! you wouldn't have us absolutely merciless?

Fred.: There's my difficulty: until twelve o'clock I would, after twelve I wouldn't. Was ever a man placed in so delicate a situation? (*Ruth comes down C.*)

Ruth: And Ruth, your own Ruth, whom you love so well, and who has won her middle-aged way into your boyish heart, what is to become of *her*?

King: Oh, he will take you with him. (*Hands Ruth to Frederic.*)

Fred.: Well, Ruth, I feel some little difficulty about you. It is true that I admire you very much, but I have been constantly at sea since I was eight years old, and yours is the only woman's face I have seen during that time. I think it is a sweet face.

Ruth: It is— oh, it is!

Fred.: I say I *think* it is— that is my impression. But as I have never had an opportunity of comparing you with other women, it is just possible I may be mistaken.

King: True.

Fred.: What a terrible thing it would be if I were to marry this innocent person, and then find out that she is, on the whole, plain!

King: Oh, Ruth is very well, very well indeed.

Sam.: Yes, there are the remains of a fine woman about Ruth.

Fred.: Do you really think so?

Sam.: I do.

Fred.: Then I will not be so selfish as to take her from you. In justice to her and in consideration for you, I will leave her behind. (*Hands Ruth to King.*)

King: No, Frederic, this must not be. We are rough men, who lead a rough life, but we are not so utterly heartless as to deprive thee of thy love. I think I am right in saying that there is not one here who would rob thee of this inestimable treasure for all the world holds dear.

All: (*loudly*) Not one!

King: No, I thought there wasn't. Keep thy love, Frederic, keep thy love. (*Hands her back to Fred.*)

Fred.: You're very good, I'm sure. (*Exit Ruth.*)

King: Well, it's the top of the tide, and we must be off. Farewell, Frederic. When your process of extermination begins, let our deaths be as swift and painless as you can conveniently make them.

Fred.: I will. By the love I have for you, I swear it. Would that you could render this extermination unnecessary by accompanying me back to civilization!

King: No, Frederic, it cannot be. I don't think much of our profession; but, contrasted with respectability, it is comparatively honest. No, Frederic, I shall live and die a Pirate King.

No. 3. "Oh, better far to live and die"

Solo and Chorus

Pirate King and Pirates

23

38710

(Pause 2nd verse only)

is, it is a glo-rious thing To be a Pi - rate King!

It is! Hur-

Hur-rah for the Pi - rate King!___

rah for our Pi - rate King! Hur-rah for the Pi - rate King!___

(Exeunt R. and R.U.E., all except Frederic. Enter Ruth. Frederic comes down C., followed by Ruth.)

38710

Ruth: Oh, take me with you! I cannot live if I am left behind.

Fred.: Ruth, I will be quite candid with you. You are very dear to me, as you know, but I must be circumspect. You see, you are considerably older than I. A lad of twenty-one usually looks for a wife of seventeen.

Ruth: A wife of seventeen! You will find me a wife of a thousand!

Fred.: No, but I shall find you a wife of forty-seven, and that is quite enough. Ruth, tell me candidly and without reserve: compared with other women, how are *you*?

Ruth: I will answer you truthfully, master: I have a slight cold, but otherwise I am quite well.

Fred.: I am sorry for your cold, but I was referring rather to your personal appearance. Compared with other women, are you beautiful?

Ruth: *(bashfully)* I have been told so, dear master.

Fred.: Ah, but lately?

Ruth: Oh, no; years and years ago.

Fred.: What do you think of yourself?

Ruth: It is a delicate question to answer, but I think I am a fine woman.

Fred.: That is your candid opinion?

Ruth: Yes, I should be deceiving you if I told you otherwise.

Fred.: Thank you, Ruth. I believe you, for I am sure you would not practise on my inexperience. I wish to do the right thing, and if — I say, *if* — you are really a fine woman, your age shall be no obstacle to our union! *(Shakes hands with her. Chorus of girls heard in the distance, "climbing over rocky mountain", etc. See entrance of girls.)* Hark! Surely I hear voices! Who has ventured to approach our all but inaccessible lair? Can it be Custom House? No, it does not sound like Custom House.

Ruth: *(aside)* Confusion! it is the voices of young girls! If he should see them I am lost.

Fred.: *(climbing rocky arch R. C. and looking off L.)* By all that's marvellous, a bevy of beautiful maidens!

Ruth: *(aside)* Lost! lost! lost!

Fred.: How lovely, how surpassingly lovely, is the plainest of them! What grace — what delicacy — what refinement! And Ruth — Ruth told me she was beautiful!

No. 4. "Oh, false one, you have deceived me!"
Recitative and Duet
Frederic and Ruth

I have de-ceived you? Yes, de-ceived me! You

told me you were fair as gold! And, mas-ter, am I

not so? And now I see you're plain and old. I'm

sure I'm not a jot so. Up-on my in-no-

cence you play. I'm not the one to plot so. Your

face is lined, your hair is grey. It's grad - u - al - ly

B Fred.

got so. Faith - less wo - man to de - ceive me, I who

Ruth

trust - ed so! Mas - ter, mas - ter, do not leave me, Hear me, ere you

Fred. **Ruth** **Fred.** **Ruth**

go! Faith - less wo - man! Mas - ter, master! Faith - less wo - man! Mas - ter,

master, do not leave me, do not leave me, Hear me, ere you

Fred.
Faith - less wo - man to de - ceive me, I who trust - ed

go! Mas - ter, mas - ter, do not leave me, Hear me, ere

so! Faith-less wo - man to de - ceive me, I who trust -

you go!

- ed so!

(At the end he renounces her, and she goes off R. in despair.)

go!

so!

Recit. **Fred.**

What shall I do? Be - fore these gen - tle maid - ens I

dare not show in this a - larm - ing cos - tume! No, no, I must re - main in close con -

(Hides in cave as they enter from R. and L., climbing over the rocks at L. of the stage and through arched rock R.)

ceal - ment Un - til I can ap - pear in de - cent cloth - ing.

No. 5. "Climbing over rocky mountain"

Chorus and Solos

Girls, Edith, and Kate

Chorus of Girls

Climb-ing o - ver rock-y moun-tain, Skip-ping riv-u - let and foun-tain,

Scal-ing rough and rug-ged pass-es, Climb the har - dy_ lit - tle lass-es,

Till_ the_ bright sea - shore they gain;

Scal-ing rough and rug-ged pass-es, Climb the har-dy_ lit - tle lass-es,

cresc.

Till_ the_ bright sea - shore they gain!

Edith

Let us gai-ly tread the__ mea-sure, Make the most of fleet-ing__ lei-sure, Hail it as__ a__ true al - ly, Though it per-ish__ by - and- by.

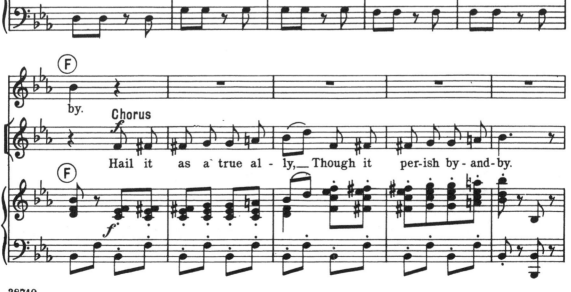

Chorus

Hail it as a true al - ly,__ Though it per-ish by-and-by.

die, Greet them gai-ly as they fly.

H Kate

Far a - way from toil and care,

Rev - el - ling in fresh sea - air, Here we live and reign a -

lone In a world that's all our own. Here, in this our

rock - y den Far a - way from mor - tal men, We'll be

queens, and make de - crees— They may hon - our them who

please. **Chorus**

We'll be queens, and make de - crees— They may hon-our them who please.

Tutti

Let us gai - ly tread the ___ mea - sure, Make the

most of fleet - ing___ lei - sure, Hail it as a

true al - ly, Though it per - ish___ by - and - by,

Hail it as a true al - ly, Though it per - ish___

by - and - by. Let us gai - ly___ tread the mea-sure, Make the most of___

38710

fleet-ing lei-sure, Hail it as a true al-ly, a true_____

al - ly.

Kate: What a picturesque spot! I wonder where we are!

Edith: And I wonder where Papa is. We have left him ever so far behind.

Isabel: Oh, he will be here presently! Remember poor Papa is not as young as we are, and we came over a rather difficult country.

Kate: But how thoroughly delightful it is to be so entirely alone! Why, in all probability we are the first human beings who ever set foot on this enchanting spot.

Isabel: Except the mermaids – it's the very place for mermaids.

Kate: Who are only human beings down to the waist–

Edith: And who can't be said strictly to set *foot* anywhere. Tails they may, but feet they *cannot.*

Kate: But what shall we do until Papa and the servants arrive with the luncheon? *(All listen and come down.)*

Edith: We are quite alone, and the sea is as smooth as glass. Suppose we take off our shoes and stockings and paddle?

All: Yes, yes! The very thing! *(They prepare to carry out the suggestion. They have all taken off one shoe, when Frederic comes forward from cave.)*

No. 6. "Stop, ladies, pray!"

Recitative and Chorus

Frederic, Edith, Kate, and Girls

No. 7. "Oh, is there not one maiden breast"

Solos and Chorus

Frederic, Mabel, and Girls

No. 8. "Poor wandering one!"
Solo and Chorus
Mabel and Girls

Ⓑ f Chorus of Girls

Take heart, no dan-ger low'rs; Take an - y heart— but ours!

Mabel

Take heart, fair days will shine; Take an - y heart— take mine!

f Chorus

Take heart, no dan-ger low'rs; Take___ an - y

heart— but ours! Take heart, fair days will shine; Take an - y

heart— take mine! Ah!_____ Ah!_____ Ah!_

cresc.

Ah!_____

f

D *a tempo*

Poor   wan - d'ring one!_____   Tho' thou hast sure - ly   stray'd,

p a tempo

Take heart of   grace,   Thy steps re - trace,   Poor_   wan - d'ring

Take___ mine! Take___ heart!_____

Chorus

Take an - y heart— but ours!

Take heart!

Take heart!

Take

No. 9. "What ought we to do"

Solos and Chorus

Edith, Kate, and Girls

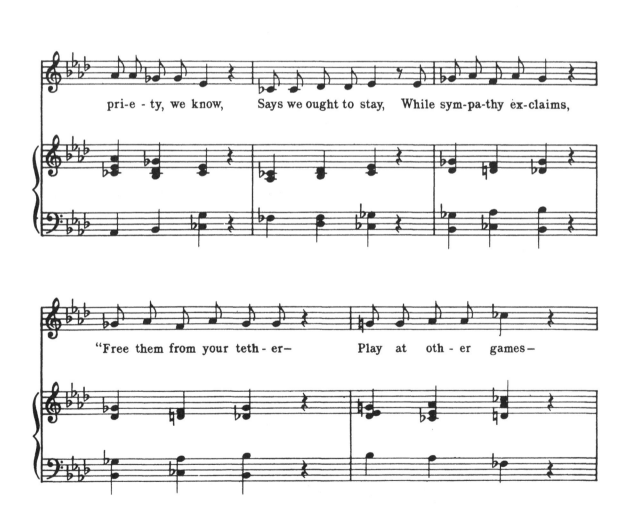

Allegretto   Edith

What ought we to do,   Gen-tle sis-ters, say?   Pro-

pri-e-ty, we know,   Says we ought to stay,   While sym-pa-thy ex-claims,

"Free them from your teth-er—   Play at oth-er games—

Leave them here to-geth-er." Her case may, an-y day, Be

yours, my dear, or mine. Let her make her hay While the sun doth shine.

Let us com-pro-mise (Our hearts are not of leath-er): Let us shut our eyes And

talk a-bout the weath-er. Yes, yes, let's talk a-bout the weath-er.

(Edith, Kate, and girls retire up, and sit two and two, facing each other, in a line across the stage.)

Attacca

No. 10. "How beautifully blue the sky"

Chattering Chorus and Duet

Girls, Mabel, and Frederic

dream_ of home - - ly du - ty To

know not why, That we shall have a warm Ju - ly.

find her day - light break With such ex - ceed - ing beau-ty?

B Did ev - er maid - en close Her eyes on wak - ing sad-ness,

To dream of such _____ ex - ceed - ing glad-ness?

Fred. **C** Ah, yes! ah, yes! ___ this is ___ ex - ceed - ing

38710

(Fred. and Mabel turn and see that the girls are listening; detected, they continue their chatter, forte.)

Chorus

glad-ness. How beau-ti-ful-ly blue the sky, The

glass is ris-ing ver-y high, Con-tin-ue fine I hope it may, And

yet it rained but yes-ter-day. To-mor-row it may pour a-gain (I

hear the coun-try wants some rain) Yet peo-ple say, I know not why, That

we shall have a warm Ju-ly, To-mor-row it may pour a-gain (I

64

38710

sake— his hid - - eous mis - sion

ver-y high, Con-tin-ue fine I hope it may, And yet it rained but

To find her day - light break With

To find him - self— be - trothed to

yes-ter-day. To - mor-row it may pour a - gain (I hear the coun-try

such— ex - ceed - - - ing

la . - dy of_____ po -

wants some rain) Yet peo - ple say, I know not why, That

38710

66

38710

No. 11. "Stay, we must not lose our senses"

Recitative and Chorus

Frederic, Girls, and Pirates

68

married with im - pu - ni - ty, And in - dulge in the fe -

lic - i - ty Of un - bound - ed do - mes - tic - i - ty. You shall

quick - ly be par - son - i - fied, Con - ju - gal - ly mat - ri -

mo - ni - fied, By a doc - tor of di - vin - i - ty Who is lo -

cat - ed in this vi - cin - i - ty.

Girls Ⓐ

We have missed our op - por -

p

doctor of divinity, Who resides in this vicinity,
By a doctor, a doctor, a doctor of divinity, of divinity.

Attacca

No. 12. "Hold, monsters!"

Recitative and Chorus

Mabel, Samuel, Major-General, Girls, and Pirates

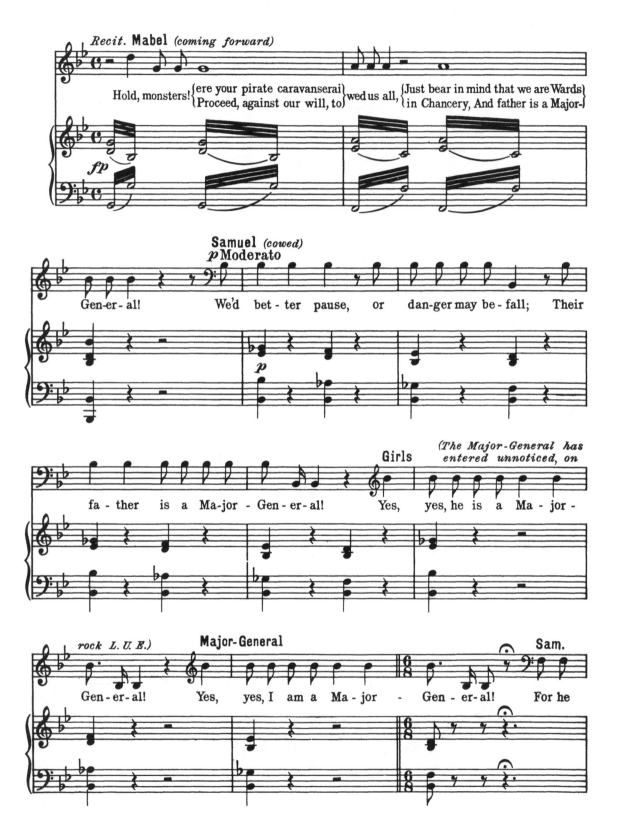

74

No. 13. "I am the very model of a modern Major-General"

Solo and Chorus

Major-General, Girls, and Pirates

Major-General

1. I am the ver-y mod-el of a mod-ern Ma-jor-Gen-er-al; I've
2. I know our myth-ic his-to-ry, King Ar-thur's and Sir Car-a-doc's; I

in-for-ma-tion veg-e-ta-ble, an-i-mal, and min-er-al: I
an-swer hard a-cros-tics; I've a pret-ty taste for par-a-dox; I

know the kings of Eng-land, and I quote the fights his - tor - i - cal, From
quote, in el - e - gi - acs, all the crimes of He - lio - gab - a - lus; In

Mar - a - thon to Wa - ter - loo, in or - der cat - e - gor - i - cal; I'm
con - ics I can floor pe - cu - li - ar - i - ties pa - rab - o - lous; I can

ver - y well ac-quaint-ed, too, with mat - ters math - e - mat - i - cal, I
tell un - doubt-ed Ra - pha - els from Ger - ard Dows and Zof - fa - nies I

un - der - stand e - qua-tions, both the sim - ple and quad-rat - i - cal, A -
know the croak-ing cho - rus from the *Frogs* of Ar - is - toph - a - nes! Then

bout bi - no - mial the - o - rem I'm teem-ing with a lot o' news,
I can hum a fugue of which I've heard the mu - sic's din a - fore,

al has nev-er *sat a, sat a* gee.

Major

4. For my

al has nev-er *sat a, sat a* gee.

fz

mil - i - ta - ry know-ledge, tho' I'm pluck-y and ad - ven-tur-y, Has

pp

on - ly been brought down to the be - gin-ning of the cen-tu-ry; But

still, in mat-ters veg-e-ta - ble, an - i - mal, and min-er - al, I

38710

Major: And now that I've introduced myself, I should like to have some idea of what's going on.

Kate: Oh, Papa—we—

Sam.: Permit me, I'll explain in two words: we propose to marry your daughters.

Major: Dear me!

Girls: Against our wills, Papa—against our wills!

Major: Oh, but you mustn't do that! May I ask—this is a picturesque uniform, but I'm not familiar with it. What are you?

King: We are all single gentlemen.

Major: Yes, I gathered that. Anything else?

King: No, nothing else.

Edith: Papa, don't believe them; they are pirates—the famous Pirates of Penzance!

Major: The Pirates of Penzance! I have often heard of them.

Mabel: All except this gentleman (*indicating Frederic*), who was a pirate once, but who is out of his indentures to-day, and who means to lead a blameless life evermore.

Major: But wait a bit. I object to pirates as sons-in-law.

King: We object to major-generals as fathers-in-law. But we waive that point. We do not press it. We look over it.

Major: (*aside*) Hah! an idea! (*Aloud* And do you mean to say that you would deliberately rob me of these, the sole remaining props of my old age, and leave me to go through the remainder of my life unfriended, unprotected, and alone?

King: Well, yes, that's the idea.

Major: Tell me, have you ever known what it is to be an orphan?

Pirates: (*disgusted*) Oh, dash it all!

King: Here we are again!

Major: I ask you, have you ever known what it is to be an orphan?

King: (*sighing*) Often!

Major: Yes, orphan. Have you ever known what it is to be one?

King: I say, often.

All: (*disgusted*) Often, often, often. (*Turning away*)

Major: I don't think we quite understand one another. I ask you, have you ever known what it is to be an orphan, and you say "orphan". As I understand you, you are merely repeating the word "orphan" to show that you understand me.

King: I didn't repeat the word often.

Major: Pardon me, you did indeed.

King: I only repeated it once.

Major: True, but you repeated it.

King: But not often.

Major: Stop! I think I can see where we are getting confused. When you said "orphan", did you mean "orphan", a person who has lost his parents, or "often", frequently!

King: Ah! I beg pardon—I see what you mean—frequently.

Major: Ah! you said "often", frequently.

King: No, only once.

Major: (*irritated*) Exactly—you said "often, frequently" only once.

No. 14. "Oh, men of dark and dismal fate"

Finale of Act I

Ensemble

Allegro vivace

Major *(aside)*

I'm tell-ing a ter-ri-ble sto-ry, But it doesn't di-min-ish my glo-ry; For they would have tak-en my daugh-ters O-ver the bil-low-y wa-ters, If I had-n't, in el-e-gant dic-tion, In-dulged in an in-no-cent fic-tion, Which is not in the same cat-e-go-ry As tell-ing a reg-u-lar ter-ri-ble

tend to di-min-ish his glo - ry; Though they would have tak- en his

tend to di-min-ish his glo - ry; Though they would have tak- en his

die by a death that is go - ry, Yes, one of the cru-el-lest

die by a death that is go - ry, Yes, one of the cru-el-lest

die by a death that is go - ry, Yes, one of the cru-el-lest

tend to di-min-ish his glo - ry; Though they would have tak- en his

die by a death that is go - ry, Yes, one of the cru-el-lest

38710

94

38710

reg-u-lar sto - ry.

reg-u-lar sto - ry.

reg-u-lar sto - ry.

reg-u-lar sto - ry.

reg-u-lar sto - ry.

reg-u-lar sto - ry.

reg- u-lar sto - ry.

Moderato   King

Al- though our dark ca - reer Some-times in - volves the crime of

steal-ing,   We   rath - er think that we're Not al - to - geth-er void of

feel-ing.   Al - though we live   by   strife, We're al - ways   sor - ry to be-

gin it;   For what, we ask, is   life Without a   touch of Poetry in it?

D (All kneel)

be!

Should it be-

be!

Should it be-

be!

Should it be-

be!

Should it be-

be!

Should it be-

Oh, hap-py day, with joy - ous glee They will a - way and mar-ried be!

Oh, hap-py day, with joy - ous glee They will a - way and mar-ried be!

104

38710

lee, My sis-ters all will bridesmaids be! My sis-ters

lee, Her sis-ters all will bridesmaids be! Her sis-ters

lee, Her sis-ters all will bridesmaids be! Her sis-ters

lee, Her sis-ters all will bridesmaids be! Her sis-ters

lee, Her sis-ters all will bridesmaids be! Her sis-ters

lee, Should it be-fall aus-pi-cious-lee, Her sis-ters

lee, Should it be-fall aus-pi-cious-lee, Her sis-ters

lee, Should it be-fall aus-pi-cious-lee, Her sis-ters

all will brides-maids be!____

all will brides-maids be!____

all will brides-maids be!____

all will brides-maids be!____

all will brides-maids be!____

all will brides-maids be!____

all will brides-maids be!____

all will brides-maids be!____

Fred., Sam., King, Major, & Pirates

Pray ob-serve the mag-na - nim-i - ty   We dis-play to lace and

dim-i - ty!   Nev-er was such op-por - tu - ni-ty   To get mar-ried with im-

pu-ni-ty!   But we give up the fe - lic-i-ty   Of un-bound-ed do - mes-

tic-i-ty,   Tho' a doc-tor of di - vin-i-ty   Is lo-cat-ed in this vi -

110

28710

Men with Pirates, *p*
as before

Mabel with Sop.
Edith & Kate
with Altos

sides in this vi - cin-i -ty, Tho'a doc-tor, a doc-tor, re - sides in this vi -

sides in this vi - cin-i-ty, Tho'a doc-tor, a doc-tor, re - sides in this vi -

cin-i-ty,　this vi - cin-i-ty.

cin-i-ty,　this vi - cin-i-ty.

Tempo primo

(Girls and Major-General go up rocks L.,

while Pirates indulge in a wild dance of delight on stage R. and R.C. The Major-General pro-

duces a British flag, and the Pirate King, in arched rock R.C., produces a black flag with skull and crossbones. Enter Ruth, who makes a final appeal to Frederic, who casts her from him.)

Act II

Scene: *A ruined chapel by moonlight. Aisles C., R., and L., divided by pillars and arches, ruined Gothic windows at back. Major-General Stanley discovered seated R. C. pensively, surrounded by his daughters.*

No. 15. "Oh, dry the glistening tear"
Opening Chorus and Solo
Girls and Mabel

creep,— For oh, they can-not bear To see their fa - - ther weep!

(Enter Mabel) Mabel

Dear fa-ther, why leave your bed At this un-time-ly hour, When hap - py day-light is dead And dark - some dan - gers low'r?— See, heav'n has lit— her lamp, The mid-night hour is past, And the chil - ly night-air is damp, The

dew is fall-ing fast! Dear fa-ther, why leave your bed When hap-py

day-light is dead?

Chorus of Girls

Oh, dry the glis-t'ning tear That dews that mar-tial cheek,— Thy

lov-ing chil-dren hear, In them thy com-fort seek. With

sym-pa-thet-ic care Their arms a-round— thee— creep,— For

oh, they can-not bear To see their fa - ther weep!___

(Frederic enters R.U.E. and down C.)

Mabel: Oh, Frederic, cannot you, in the calm excellence of your wisdom, reconcile it with your conscience to say something that will relieve my father's sorrow?

Fred.: I will try, dear Mabel. But why does he sit, night after night, in this draughty old ruin?

Major: Why do I sit here? To escape from the pirates' clutches, I described myself as an orphan; and, heaven help me, I am no orphan! I came here to humble myself before the tombs of my ancestors, and to implore their pardon for having brought dishonour on the family escutcheon.

Fred.: But you forget, sir, you only bought the property a year ago, and the stucco on your baronial castle is scarcely dry.

Major: Frederic, in this chapel are ancestors: you cannot deny that. With the estate, I bought the chapel and its contents. I don't know whose ancestors they *were*, but I know whose ancestors they *are*, and I shudder to think that their descendant by purchase (if I may so describe myself) should have brought disgrace upon what, I have no doubt, was an unstained escutcheon.

Fred.: Be comforted. Had you not acted as you did, these reckless men would assuredly have called in the nearest clergyman, and have married your large family on the spot.

Major: I thank you for your proffered solace, but it is unavailing. I assure you, Frederic, that such is the anguish and remorse I feel at the abominable falsehood by which I escaped these easily deluded pirates, that I would go to their simple-minded chief this very night and confess all, did I not fear that the consequences would be most disastrous to myself. At what time does your expedition march against these scoundrels?

Fred.: At eleven, and before midnight I hope to have atoned for my involuntary association with the pestilent scourges by sweeping them from the face of the earth— and then, dear Mabel, you will be mine!

Major: Are your devoted followers at hand?

Fred.: They are; they only wait my orders.

No. 16. "Then, Frederic, let your escort lion-hearted"

Recitative

Major-General and Frederic

Major

Then, Fred-er-ic, let your es-cort li-on-heart-ed Be sum-moned to re-ceive a gen'ral's bless-ing

Ere they de-part up-on their dread ad-ven-ture.

Fred.

Dear sir, they

No. 17. "When the foeman bares his steel"

Solos and Chorus

Sergeant, Mabel, Edith, Major-General, Police, and Girls

Allegro marziale *(Enter Police, marching in single file from L., 2nd E., and*

come.

form in line, facing audience.)

Sergeant

When the foe-man bares his steel,

Chorus of Police (using their

Ta-ran-ta-

We un-com-fort-a-ble feel,

clubs as trumpets)

ra, ta-ran-ta-ra! Ta-ran-ta-

And we find the wis-est thing Is to

ra! Ta-ran-ta-ra, ta-ran-ta-ra!

122

38710

ten-tions are well meant,   Such ex-pres-sions don't ap-pear

Ta-ran-ta - ra!   Ta-ran-ta-

Cal-cu-lat - ed men to cheer   Who are

ra, ta-ran-ta-ra!   Ta-ran - ta - ra!

going to meet their fate   In   a   high - ly ner - vous state.

Ta-ran - ta-

Still, to   us   it's ev - i-dent These at-

ra, ta-ran-ta-ra, ta-ran - ta - ra!

ten - tions are well meant.

Ta - ran - ta - ra, ta - ran - ta - ra, ta - ran - ta-

Edith *(from R., addressing Sergeant)*

ra!   Go,_____ and do your

best_____ en - deav - our. And_____ be - fore all links we

sev - 3 er,   We_____ will say fare - well_____ for ev - er.

cresc.

risks that on us press, And of ref - er-ence a lack To our

chance of com - ing back. Still, per - haps it would be wise Not to

pp

carp or crit - i - cise, For it's ver - y ev - i - dent These at-

ten-tions are well meant.

Yes, it's ver - y ev - i - dent

Police

Ev - i -

These at - ten-tions are well meant,

go, at last they go, at last they go! At last they real - ly

go, at last they go, at last they go! At last they real - ly, real - ly

go, at last they go, at last they go! At last they real - ly, real - ly

go, we go, we go! We go, we go, we go, we

go, we go, we go! We go, we go, we go, we

At last they go, at last they go! At last they real - ly, real - ly

(Exeunt Police. Mabel tears herself from Fred., and exits R., followed by her sisters, consoling her. The Major-General and others follow the police off L. Fred. remains alone.)

go!

go!

go!

go!

go!

go!

No. 18. "Now for the pirates' lair!"
Recitative

Frederic, Pirate King, and Ruth

140

38710

No. 19. "When you had left our pirate fold"

Solos, Trio, and Chant

Ruth, Frederic, and Pirate King

all in vain the quips we heard; We lay and sobbed up - on the rocks, Un-

said, "If we could tell it him, How Fred -'ric would the joke en - joy!" And

Fred.

til to some - bod - y oc - curred A start - ling par - a - dox. A par - a -

Fred. *(interested)*

so we've risked both life and limb To tell it to our boy. That par - a -

p

Ruth *(laughing)*

dox? A par - a - dox, A most in - ge - nious par - a - dox! We've quips and

King *(laughing)*

dox? That par - a - dox, That most in - ge - nious par - a - dox! We've quips and

Ⓑ

quib - bles heard in flocks, But none to beat this par - a - dox!

quib - bles heard in flocks, But none to beat this par - a - dox!

Ⓑ

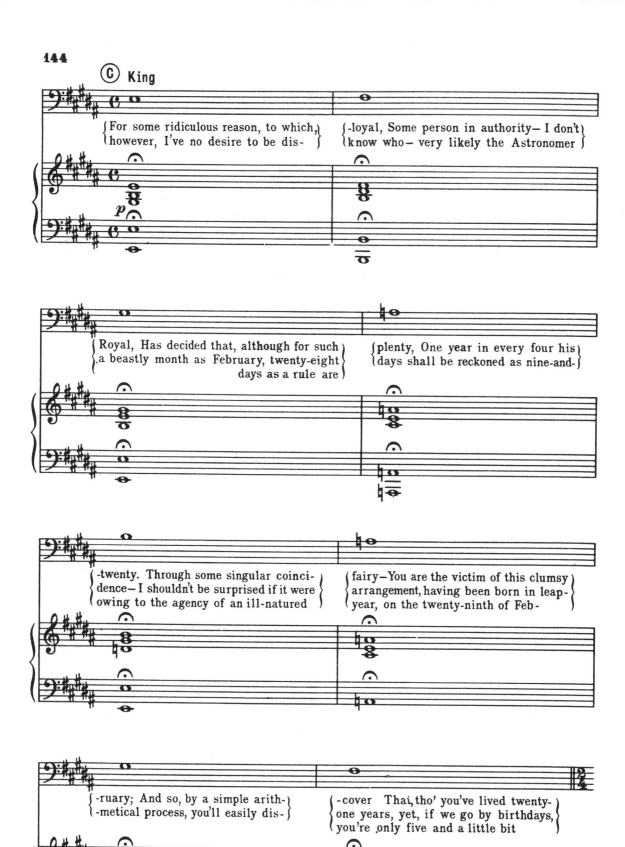

Ⓒ King

For some ridiculous reason, to which, however, I've no desire to be dis- -loyal, Some person in authority— I don't know who— very likely the Astronomer

Royal, Has decided that, although for such a beastly month as February, twenty-eight days as a rule are plenty, One year in every four his days shall be reckoned as nine-and-

-twenty. Through some singular coinci- dence— I shouldn't be surprised if it were owing to the agency of an ill-natured fairy—You are the victim of this clumsy arrangement, having been born in leap- year, on the twenty-ninth of Feb-

-ruary; And so, by a simple arith- -metical process, you'll easily dis- -cover That, tho' you've lived twenty- one years, yet, if we go by birthdays, you're only five and a little bit

38710

Fred.: Upon my word, this is most curious— most absurdly whimsical. Five and a quarter! No one would think it to look at me!

Ruth: You are glad now, I'll be bound, that you spared us. You would never have forgiven yourself when you discovered that you had killed *two of your comrades.*

Fred.: My comrades?

King: *(rises)* I'm afraid you don't appreciate the delicacy of your position. You were apprenticed to us—

Fred.: Until I reached my twenty-first year.

King: No, until you reached your twenty-first birthday *(producing document)*, and, going by birthdays, you are as yet only five and a quarter.

Fred.: You don't mean to say you are going to hold me to that?

King: No, we merely remind you of the fact, and leave the rest to your sense of duty.

Ruth: *(rises)* Your sense of duty!

Fred.: *(wildly)* Don't put it on that footing! As I was merciful to you just now, be merciful to me! I implore you not to insist on the letter of your bond just as the cup of happiness is at my lips!

Ruth: We insist on nothing; we content ourselves with pointing out to you *your duty.*

King: Your duty!

Fred.: *(after a pause)* Well, you have appealed to my sense of duty, and my duty is only too clear. I abhor your infamous calling; I shudder at the thought that I have ever been mixed up with it; but duty is before all— at any price I will do my duty.

King: Bravely spoken! Come, you are one of us once more.

Fred.: Lead on, I follow! *(Suddenly.)* Oh, horror!

King:⎫ What is the matter?
Ruth:⎭

Fred.: Ought I to tell you? No, no, I cannot do it; and yet, as one of your band—

King: Speak out, I charge you by that sense of conscientiousness to which we have never yet appealed in vain.

Fred.: General Stanley, the father of my Mabel—

King:⎫ Yes, yes!
Ruth:⎭

Fred.: He escaped from you on the plea that he was an orphan?

King: He did.

Fred.: It breaks my heart to betray the honoured father of the girl I adore, but as your apprentice I have no alternative. It is my duty to tell you that General Stanley is no orphan.

King:⎫ What!
Ruth:⎭

Fred.: More than that, he never was one!

King: Am I to understand that, to save his contemptible life, he dared to practise on our credulous simplicity? *(Frederic nods as he weeps.)* Our revenge shall be swift and terrible. We will go and collect our band and attack Tremorden Castle this very night.

Fred.: But— stay—

King: Not a word! He is doomed!

No. 20. "Away, away! my heart's on fire"
Trio
Ruth, Pirate King, and Frederic

foul He tricked us of our brides.__ Let ven-geance howl;The pi-rate so de-

cides!__ Our na-ture stern He sof-tened with his lies;__ And, in re-

Yes, yes! to-night the trai-tor

Yes, yes! to-night the trai-tor

turn, To-night the trai - tor dies!__

No. 21. "All is prepared"

Recitative

Mabel and Frederic

til I reached my one and twen-tieth birth - day— But you

are twen-ty - one? I've just dis - cov - ered That I was born in

leap-year, and that birth-day Will not be reached by me till nine - teen

for-ty! Oh, hor - ri-ble! ca - tas-tro-phe ap-pall-ing! And

so, fare - well! No, no! Ah, Fred-'ric, hear me!

No. 22. "Stay, Frederic, stay!"

Duet

Mabel and Frederic

palls; But when stern Du-ty calls, I must o-bey.

A
Stay, Fred-'ric, stay! They have no claim—

A
Nay, Ma-bel, nay! But Du-ty's

No shad-ow of a shame Will fall__ up-on thy name.

name. The thought__ my soul ap-palls; But when__ stern Du-ty calls,

Mabel
Stay, Fred-'ric, stay!

Fred.
I must o-bey.

Oh, here is love, and here is truth,

here is truth, She

He will be faith-ful to his sooth,

will be faith-ful to her sooth, Till we are wed, and e - ven

Till we are wed, yes, e - ven af - -

af - ter, and e - ven af-ter!

cresc.

No. 23. "No, I am brave!"

Recitative, Solo, and Chorus

Mabel, Sergeant, and Police

172

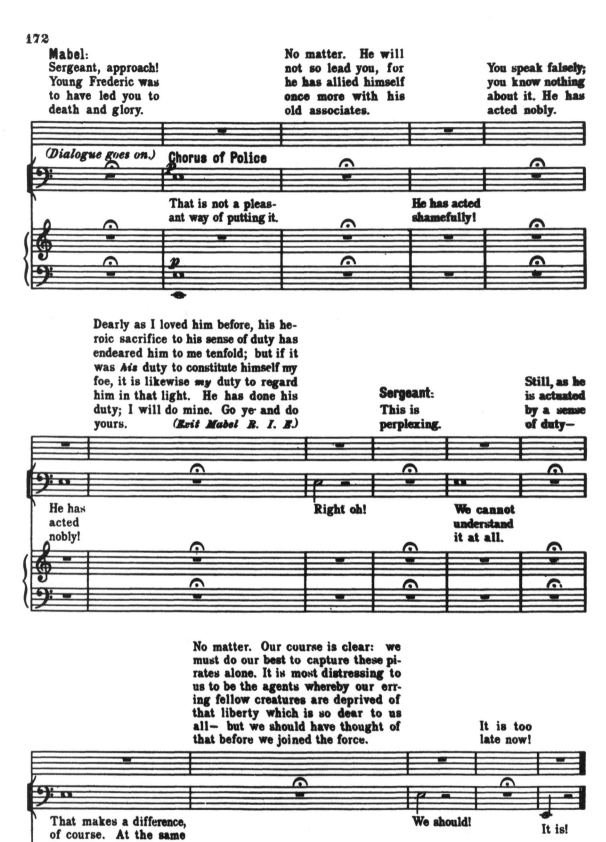

38710

Allegro

No. 24. "When a felon's not engaged in his employment"
Solo and Chorus
Sergeant and Police

stab - u - la - ry du - ty's to be done.
loves to lie a - bask - ing in the sun.
Ah, take

to be done.
in the sun.

one con - sid - er - a - tion with an - oth - er,
A po -

with an - oth - er,

lice - man's lot is not a hap - py one.
When con -

Ah, when con -

No. 25. "A rollicking band of pirates we"
Chorus and Solo
Pirates, Sergeant, and Police

seek a pen-al-ty fif-ty-fold, For Gen-er-al Stan-ley's

seek a pen-al-ty fif-ty-fold, For Gen-er-al Stan-ley's

sto - ry!

sto - ry!

Sergeant

They come in force, With stealth-y stride;

pp

Chorus of Police *repeat this, and*
pp dim. till next Chorus.

Our ob-vious course is now— to hide. Ta-ran-ta-ra, ta-ran-ta-ra!

(Police conceal themselves in aisle L. As they do so, the Pirates, with Ruth and Fred, are seen appearing at ruined window. They enter cautiously and come downstage on tiptoe. Sam, is laden with burglarious tools and pistols, etc.)

38710

No. 26. "With cat-like tread, upon our prey we steal"

Chorus and Solo

Pirates, Police, and Samuel

So stealth-i-ly the pi-rate creeps, While all the house-hold sound-ly sleeps.

ra, ta-ra - ta - ra!

Come, friends, who plough the sea,

Ra, ra, ra, ra, ra, ra, ra, ra,

on our prey we steal; In si-lence dread, Our cau-tious way we feel.

No sound at all! We nev-er speak a word; A fly's foot-fall Would be dis-

tinct - ly heard! Come, friends, who plough the sea,

pp Police

Ta-ran - ta-ra, ra, ra, ra, ra, ra, ra, ra,

Truce to nav - i - ga - tion; Take an-oth-er sta - tion; Let's va - ry

ra, ra, ra, ra, ra, ra, ra, ra, ra, ra, ra, ra,

No. 27. "Hush, hush! not a word"

Recitative, Chorus, and Solo

Frederic, Pirates, Police, and Major-General

lay up-on my sleep-less bed, And tossed and turned and groaned. The

man who finds his con-science ache No peace at all en-joys; And

Chorus of Pirates & Police *p*

as I lay in bed a-wake, I thought I heard a noise. He

Recit. **Major**

thought he heard a noise— Ha, ha! No, all is still In dale, on hill; My mind is set at

ease— So still the scene, It must have been The sigh-ing of the

No. 28. "Sighing softly to the river"
Ballad and Finale of Act II
Major-General and Ensemble

194

(Enter the Major-General's daughters, led by Mabel, all in white peignoirs and nightcaps, and carrying lighted candles.)

38710

go to bed at half-past ten. What strange oc‑cur‑rence can it be that

calls dear fa‑ther from his rest At such a time of night as this, so

ver‑y in‑com‑plete‑ly dressed? So

ver‑y in‑com‑plete‑ly dressed, at such a time of

(Enter King, Sam., and Fred.)

King: Forward, my men, and seize that general there! His life is over.

night!

(They seize the Major-General.) Girls

The

pi - rates! the pi - rates! Oh, de - spair!

Pirates *(springing up)*

Yes, we're the pi - rates; so de - spair!

Mabel: spare him! Will no one in his cause a weap-on wield? Oh,

Girls: spare him!

Police (*springing up*): Yes, we are here, though hith-er-to con-cealed! Oh,

Girls: rap-ture!

Police: So to Con-stab-u-la-ry, pi-rates yield! Oh,

Girls: rap-ture!

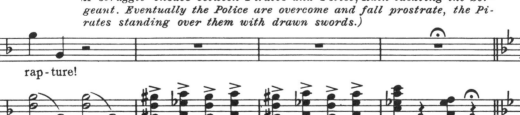

(*A struggle ensues between Pirates and Police, Ruth tackling the Sergeant. Eventually the Police are overcome and fall prostrate, the Pirates standing over them with drawn swords.*)

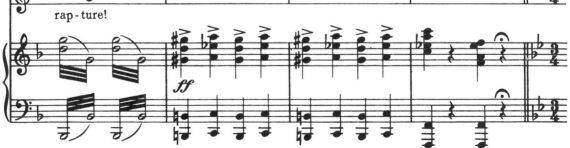

200

38710

- ah, ah, ah! Fair days will shine; Take ___ heart- ___

wan-d'ring one! Fair days will shine; Take ___ heart- ___

wan-d'ring one! Take heart, take heart,

wan-d'ring one! Take heart, take heart,

wan-d'ring one! Take heart, take heart,

wan-d'ring one! Take heart, take heart,

Take heart, take heart,

Take heart, take heart,

Take heart—

Take heart—

Take heart—

Take heart—

Take heart—

Take heart—

Take mine!

Take mine!

take ours! Take

take ours! Take

take ours! Take

take ours! Take

take ours! Take

take ours! Take

Mabel
Take heart— Take ours!

Edith
Take heart— Take ours!

Kate & Ruth
Take heart— Take ours!

King
Take heart— Take ours!

Take heart— Take ours!

Fred. with Tenor
Sam. with Bass
Take heart— Take ours!

a tempo

sempre ff

End of Opera